William Faulkner's LIGHT IN AUGUST

A CRITICAL COMMENTARY

LESLIE SHEPARD
DEPARTMENT OF COMPARATIVE LITERATURE
NEW YORK UNIVERSITY

Ethnic Vacuum

MONARCH PRESS

Published by
MONARCH PRESS
a division of Simon & Schuster, Inc.
1 West 39th Street
New York, N.Y. 10018

Standard Book Number: 671-00666-5

Library of Congress Catalog Card Number: 66-1760

Printed in the United States of America

CONTENTS

INTRODUCTION

1. THE LIFE AND WORKS OF WILLIAM FAULKNER

FAMILY BACKGROUND: No Faulkner biography can ignore his great-grandfather, Colonel William Cuthbert Falkner, who, at the age of fourteen, ran away from home to an uncle in Ripley, Mississippi, and thereby founded a branch of the family in the deep South. Colonel Falkner was a picturesque, colorful person, a source of legend and glory for succeeding generations of Falkners. A lawyer, he raised a volunteer regiment in the Civil War and fought gallantly. Later he had railroad lines built, owned a twelve-hundred-acre plantation, a cotton gin, and several mills, and finally became a best-selling author of novels and essays before he was killed by an assassin's bullet in 1889.

His son, John Wesley Thompson Falkner, was a figure of somewhat diminished brilliance when compared to his father, whose gunslinging adventures he could not match. He improved the railroad and became the president of the First National Bank at Oxford, Mississippi. He had two children, a girl and a boy, the latter named Murry.

William Faulkner (this was the original spelling of the name before his great-grandfather changed it out of contempt for the Missouri Faulkners) was the first of the four sons of Murry and his wife Maud, née Butler. William was born on September 25, 1897, at New Albany, Union County, Mississippi. When he was five years old, the family moved to Oxford, in

Lafayette County. The father, Murry, was a shiftless man, who represented a marked decline in the family's status. He never finished college, served for a time as conductor on his father's railroad, ran a hardware store, and finally became secretary and business manager at Ole Miss, the University of Mississippi, which is located in the town of Oxford.

THE AURA OF GENTEEL DECADENCE: Young William Faulkner could observe in his family the picture of gradual decline, from his great-grandfather down to his father. Though the profile of financial deterioration may have appeared more sharply in the history of the Falkner family, such decline was not unusual in that part of the country. It coincided with the line of economic development of the South and of the United States as a whole. Though the Jefferson of Faulkner's novels, Oxford's fictional counterpart, is steeped in the past, in reality this past is not very remote. The history of Lafayette County goes back to the time of the Old Colonel, when enterprising and resourceful men like William Cuthbert himself moved there. The economy of the area, then a frontier land, was based on cheap Negro labor, employed mostly in agriculture.

A generation later, the plantations of the founders came to support a new breed of men who regarded themselves as the local aristocracy and had cultural and snobbish pretensions. The Civil War and the abolition of slavery were fatal to this plantation aristocracy, at a time the industrial revolution was in full bloom in the North and West. The chivalric code of ethics as well as the feudal form of life which materially supported it were outmoded and falling into oblivion during the childhood of William Faulkner. But the imagination of the boy was fired by the heroic legends about the family's former greatness, and his loyalties were on the side of the agricultural civilization and not the developing acquisitive, unchivalric, industrialized South. For the new type was unmindful of pastoral beauties, its traditions, and the concept of the gentleman. These *nouveaux riches* were interested only in profit, probably not unlike those who, some half a century before, had founded its feudal system.

CHILDHOOD AND YOUTH: William was an occasionally thoughtful but not by any means an introverted youngster. Being the oldest, he was the ringleader of his playmates. But his most distinguishing trademark was the telling of tall stories. His gifts as a storyteller were so appreciated by the other children that they would do Billy's chores while he talked. Fact and fancy were merged in Billy's tales to such an extent that his playmates never knew just how much of them he invented.

But during his adolescence a great change was taking place in William's character. He read more and more, lost interest in sports. He went for long walks across the countryside, neglected his scholastic duties. He began to write poetry. By the time he was seventeen, he had dropped out of high school. Indications were that the Falkners' transformation from doers into dreamers would culminate in William.

When the news spread that young Faulkner had engaged himself on the path of literary perdition, the family summoned Philip Stone, a young man of twenty-one, who enjoyed the reputation of being something of a *littérateur,* to come and read Billy's poems. Stone appeared, pored over seventeen-year-old Billy's recent production, and forthwith declared him to be a genius. This was the beginning of a long and devoted friendship, during which Stone fostered Faulkner's intellectual development and enthusiastically tried to promote his literary career. Though Stone was preparing to be a lawyer, he was well read, and his real interests were literary. They spent many hours together, discussing history and literature, taking walks, immersing themselves in the lore and natural beauty of the South.

In 1918 Stone went to Yale, and Faulkner decided to enroll in the Army. But he was turned down, being too short. Undaunted, he enlisted in the Royal Canadian Air Force. It was too late in the war for him to see much action, and the stories of Faulkner's gallantry can be safely classified as part of his fiction. The leg injury he sustained was caused by a drunken escapade on Armistice Day.

Returning home, the wounded warrior enrolled as a special student at the University of Mississippi, though he had not graduated from high school. He started with great enthusiasm, but in the face of the drudgery of the student's daily routine his initial enthusiasm waned, and a year later Faulkner quit. He hoped that writing could be his means of support, and with this objective in mind turned from poetry to short stories. He and Stone sent them out to magazines where they were invariably rejected. Seeing that he was totally unsuccessful and doubtful of his vocation as a writer, Faulkner began to adopt the habits of an intellectual hobo. He walked barefoot, did not shave, and wore soiled clothes. He spent his days loitering about in the courthouse square, listening to stories, daydreaming, living on odd jobs.

Stone, who would periodically come up with an idea to launch Faulkner on his belated career, suggested that he go to New York City to establish contact with the literary world there. He traveled to New York in 1923 but made no headway and returned in the same year. For a time he served as postmaster at Ole Miss. His record in this field of endeavor is not distinguished. He fitted the postmastership into his schedule of walking, drinking, and writing as best he could, but the mail kept getting lost. In 1924 a volume of his poetry was printed, subsidized by Stone. It met with no critical or popular success.

LITERARY BREAKTHROUGH: In 1925 Faulkner was in New Orleans, looking for passage on a ship bound for Europe, when he heard that Miss Prall, an old acquaintance of his, was in town. Elizabeth Prall was an intimate friend of Sherwood Anderson, the well-known author. Miss Prall introduced Faulkner to Anderson, who took a liking to him, and adopted Faulkner as his protégé. Faulkner wrote his first novel, *Soldier's Pay,* while at New Orleans, living among the crowd of confirmed Bohemians over which Anderson presided. *Soldier's Pay* was written to please the popular taste, rather than as a vehicle of artistic expression, but Anderson hailed Faulkner as his discovery and recommended the book to his publisher. It was accepted for publication and appeared a year later.

Faulkner started working on his second novel, *Mosquitoes,* in the same year. While *Soldier's Pay* had been conceived in the *fin de siècle* tradition, *Mosquitoes* was reminiscent of Aldous Huxley's *Point Counter Point,* but its satire has been judged heavy-handed by most critics. At the same time, Faulkner contributed sketches for the New Orleans *Times-Picayune.* He also contributed to a slim volume entitled *Sherwood Anderson and Other Creoles,* which he thought to be delightfully clever and humorous, but which earned him Anderson's enmity.

Shortly thereafter Faulkner left for Europe as he had planned. He walked and cycled through France and Belgium, inspecting the battlefields, and visited parts of Italy and Switzerland. In March, 1926, *Soldier's Pay* was published. It earned some praise from the critics, but its sales were poor. *Mosquitoes,* which came out in 1927, was less well received and sold no better than *Soldier's Pay*. In his third novel, *Sartoris* (1929), Faulkner finally turned to material that he knew well. In this work he found himself as a writer. *Sartoris* is a literary recounting of the Faulkner family legend, the first of the cycle about the inhabitants of Yoknapatawpha County, and its seat, Jefferson, the fictional counterpart of Lafayette County and Oxford. Most of Faulkner's major novels and many of his stories belong to this cycle, which is not one continuous saga but a loosely connected network, with many sub-plots. But *Sartoris* still had not made a lasting impression either on the public or on the critics.

THE FIRST GREAT NOVELS: *Sartoris* convinced Faulkner that he had found the subject matter around which he should compose the bulk of his lifework, but he was now equally certain that he should stop writing with the aim of courting his audience. His next book, *The Sound and the Fury,* was born of this conviction. It is a difficult work which makes no concessions to the reader. Its technique is the stream of consciousness, then a comparatively new method. Faulkner learned it from Joyce. *The Sound and the Fury* relates the decline of a family. Its most intellectual member, Quentin, a student at Harvard, contemplates suicide as he is thinking back of his incestuous love for his sister, Candace. Quentin's search for meaning in life is similar to the quest of the protagonists of many modern novels. *The Sound and the Fury* was a great artistic success, admired by the perceptive few. Though its sales were mediocre, its critical acclaim helped to establish Faulkner as a young author of promise.

MARRIAGE AND SUCCESS: Estelle Oldham was William's childhood sweetheart. However, during Faulkner's years of wandering and jobless Bohemianism she married a lawyer at her family's insistence. But in 1927 she divorced him and came back to Oxford with her two children. Faulkner still loved her and in 1929 they were married. Faulkner agreed to provide for the children too. In the same year he wrote *As I Lay Dying*. Faulkner said that he finished the book in six weeks, and intended it to be an artistic *tour de force*. The novel indeed shows an amazing virtuosity and a consummate skill in the handling of the same stream-of-consciousness technique that the author resorted to in his previous novel. Fifteen characters tell the story in fifty-nine sections. They speak as they sense, feel, and think: each of them is on a different intellectual level. The reader must make up his mind what the objective facts were. The reading of *As I Lay Dying* is a creative experience, the author only supplies the raw materials, as it were. This book, like the previous one, had a very good reception, but did not sell many copies.

With characteristic frankness, Faulkner admitted that *Sanctuary* (1931) had been conceived to make money. He had asked himself what would sell at least 10,000 copies, and he invented a tale of horror, involving the rape of a coed, Temple Drake, by a perverted gunman, named Popeye. Temple is subsequently set up by Popeye in a Memphis house of prostitution, but the bandit is eventually tried and executed, though for a crime he did not commit. Temple becomes thoroughly deranged in the moral sense during her stay at the bordello, but finally Temple's father rescues her. This Gothic story was the foundation of the author's popular success.

Suddenly Faulkner found that he was in demand. One by one he sold the stories that had been rejected by magazines. Oxford was scandalized, even the relatives were shocked, but the money came pouring in. Faulkner was invited to come to Hollywood. For the time being, he turned down this offer, and he again turned to his more serious muse, producing *Light in August* (1932). Here the technique produces no difficulty, but the plot is complex. It centers around an illegitimate boy, Joe Christmas, who is first put in an orphanage, then is adopted by a farmer and his wife, steals her money, and runs away. Joe subsequently kills his guilt-ridden New England mistress, Joanna Burden, flees, and is pursued and almost lynched before he escapes again. But finally a young man shoots him. The characters of *Light In August* are tormented human beings, caught in a hopeless struggle between their instinct and passions on the one hand and the demands of their puritanical Presbyterianism on the other. Its "message" is that men should be more tolerant of each other.

In 1930, Faulkner purchased a run-down colonial mansion that once belonged to an Irish planter. He spent much time and effort to put it back in shape. It must have represented to him the restoration of his family to its past grandeur, though, to be sure, on a more modest scale than the Old Colonel's baronial home with its many servants. There his first daughter, Alabama, was born and died soon after. She was followed by a second daughter, Jill, to whom Faulkner was devoted. Succeeding the publication of *Sanctuary,* Faulkner made large expenditures. He owned two airplanes, and the upkeep of his mansion was costly too. In November 1932 he accepted an invitation to Hollywood. He was to work for the film industry intermittently for some fifteen years, usually when he was in need of money.

Faulkner hated Hollywood, but he was realistic about his work, and obligingly produced scripts, turned out dialogues, and supplied advice as it was required of him. Faulkner gave some humorous accounts of his cooperation in the film industry. One of these, perhaps apocryphal, stories has him reporting on location once to make a film with Tod Browning. Browning told him to go see the continuity writer, for he himself was not sure what the story was that Faulkner was supposed to write. Faulkner forthwith proceeded to see the continuity writer and asked him what the story was. The man, visibly annoyed, told Faulkner to mind his own business, go off, and write some dialogue and *then* he would be told what the story was. Faulkner went back to Browning to complain that the continuity writer would not tell him the story. Browning, furious, sent him back to see the continuity writer again, but on his way Faulkner received a telegram from Hollywood, with the message, "Faulkner is fired." Browning said he would fix that, but then there came another wire, saying, "Browning is fired."

A more positive aspect of Faulkner's collaboration was that he adapted three of his works to the screen, the last of these being *Intruder in the Dust,* which was filmed in Oxford by MGM. With his proceeds from Hollywood he bought a farm, under the illusion that it would ensure him a steady income independent of the ups and downs of contracts and the sales of his books. As he was making more and more profit as a professional writer, his literary occupation appealed to him less and less. He finally came to believe that he was a gentleman farmer whose hobby was writing. This corresponded to the philosophy of his feudal forebears whom Faulkner always regarded as his models, even though he repeatedly condemned the Southern attitude concerning Negroes and poor whites.

THE MIDDLE YEARS: *Pylon* (1935), whose main characters are a family of stunt fliers, was followed by one of Faulkner's major novels, *Absalom, Absalom!* in 1936. Here Quentin Compson of *The Sound and the Fury* reappears first before he goes to Harvard and then at Harvard, telling the story of a certain Thomas Sutpen and his family. Sutpen was a poor boy. He suffered the first humiliation of his life when he was turned away from a plantation house by a Negro slave. This gave him the ambition to become wealthy. He went to the West Indies and married a local girl, Eulalia Bon. But he learned that Eulalia had Negro blood in her and left her and their child, Charles. Sutpen returned to the States and bought a plantation. He married again, never mentioning his first wife. He had two children by Ellen Coldfield, Henry and Judith. When Henry grew up he met Charles Bon at the university. Charles met Judith too and fell in love with her. Though Henry eventually found out that he and Charles were half brothers, he did not oppose his sister's marriage to Charles until he learned that Charles was part Negro. When Charles insisted, Henry killed him.

Absalom, Absalom! is a strong indictment of Southern discrimination. The tragedy is caused by the white man's refusal to accept the Negro as an equal. It is a very forcefully written book, whose style is vehement, febrile, with incredibly complex sentences which are at times incoherent and ungrammatical. As in many of Faulkner's other books, important details are held back, elucidated in later chapters, and then given an entirely new explanation toward the end. Faulkner's circuitous prose reaches one of its heights in this novel.

The Unvanquished, which followed two years later, consists of five stories from the time of the Civil War, with young Bayard Sartoris as their protagonist. He and Ringo, his Negro friend, are involved in adventures. In the last story Bayard is a college student.

The Hamlet (1940) is the first part of the saga relating the story of the Snopeses, the evil people of Yoknapatawpha, who do not observe the gentlemanly code of conduct of the former ruling class, constantly outwit their neighbors, take advantage of their good will, and finally triumph. Faulkner believed that the South had gone to the dogs as the Snopeses were gradually replacing the Sartorises. A less repulsive member of the Snopes family is Ike the idiot who is in love with his cow. The description of this relationship comprises the tenderest section of the novel.

Go Down, Moses (1942) is actually a collection of stories woven together and united by the presence of identical themes. These themes are the sacredness of nature, man's attitude towards his fellows and towards nature, and the interrelations of the two. The most important character is Isaac McCaslin, probably a projection of Faulkner's own youthful self. Isaac learns about the beauty and laws of the wilderness from a mulatto, Sam Fathers. Sam's mother was a Negro slave, his father, a Chickasaw Indian. He comprehends nature and knows that it should not be exploited. The theme of the book is that the attitude of reverence and contemplative sagacity that characterizes Sam Fathers' relations with the physical universe should not only govern man in his dealings with others, it should be the basis of the Negro-white relationship as well.

The middle-aged Faulkner came to adopt a certain routine in life that was divided between his professional work, which he was said to do in the early hours of the morning, his duties as a family man, his tasks and chores as a farmer or more precisely, country squire, and his social and public commitments. Faulkner was a polite and considerate man, except when he felt that he was imposed upon, at which times his remarks and retorts could be absolutely deadly. He could be congenial among friends of his own choosing, but those he did not like he repulsed with arrogance. With the advance of years he began to drink somewhat heavily, often in solitude.

Faulkner was short and sturdy of build; his features had the rugged handsomeness of the outdoorsman. He looked clean-cut and robust in his middle years, due to taking care of himself, and also the result of never having done what a laborer or even a busy white-collar worker would have called an honest day's work. Later photographs of him suggest a peasant wiliness and suspicion. The face that looks both shrewd and contemplative could easily be that of a French farmer, if one discounts the effect of a somewhat stylish haircut.

LATE FAULKNER: Some critics claim that the production of the last fourteen years (1948–1962) is inferior to Faulkner's best. At any rate, it shows a difference from his earlier writing in being more didactic, offering solutions to social questions, and in being less agonized and dramatic. The first of the author's postwar novels is *Intruder In the Dust*. It is another comment on race relations. Charles Mallison cannot accept the Negro Lucas Beauchamps as an equal and, like the rest of the community, is irked by Lucas' quiet self-assurance. The townspeople imagine that their time for revenge has come when a boy is murdered. Everyone accuses Lucas of the crime and there is an attempt to lynch him. Mallison, an old lady, and Mallison's Negro companion discover that the crime was committed by the victim's own brother. When Mallison brings the truth to the surface, the people cannot face the fact that they only persecuted Lucas to expose the depravity of a "nigger."

Intruder In the Dust was subsequently (1949) produced as a motion picture, bringing Faulkner once again into the public spotlight. In the intervening years he had become a forgotten great man. Most of his books were out of print and the publishers did not see fit to reissue them. The population of Oxford, seemingly oblivious of the work's social implications, was delighted that the picture was going to be done on location. People vied with each other to "be in the movies," even though it showed them trying to lynch an innocent Negro. As a publicity stunt, MGM decided to hold the world premier in Oxford, Mississippi. With great fanfare, a parade was organized. Bands marched, awards were given for the best floats under the glare of blinding lights. There was only one missing ingredient, William Faulkner himself. The good people of Oxford, who had not paid any attention to him for the past twenty-five years, did not deplore his absence, but MGM did, for reasons of world-wide publicity. He was at last tricked into attending the premiere.

In November 1950 it was announced that William Faulkner had been awarded the 1949 Nobel prize for literature. The author first said he would not go to Stockholm for the ceremony, but he changed his mind, thinking of it as an opportunity to show Paris to his beloved daughter, Jill. His acceptance speech was hailed as "one of the great speeches of this century," though in retrospect it appears rather as a collection of dignified and praiseworthy cliches. In the next years, Faulkner's reputation grew by leaps and bounds. He was considered a giant of modern letters, an authority and a prophet to be consulted on the great issues and the future of mankind. He was feted, dined and wined, and invited as a guest speaker literally all over the world. He often declined, but just as frequently obliged, and he should not be reproached for repeating himself on occasion.

Requiem for a Nun (1951) resumes the sensational story of *Sanctuary*. Temple Drake has come back from Paris and has married Gowan Stevens. But Temple cannot escape from the temptations of her depraved past. A young brother of her former Memphis lover turns up and she is willing to leave her husband to join him. A woman by the name of Nancy Mannigee frustrates her plan to escape by murdering Temple's baby. Nancy's desperate act was an attempt to awaken Temple to the burden of her moral responsibility. Nancy is tried and condemned to die, but she is calm, believing that she has done the right thing for Temple. A three-act play is interpolated in the novel, dramatizing Nancy's trial. The moral scope of *Requiem for a Nun* is of course much wider than that of *Sanctuary*. The conclusion of the novel seems to be that man is damned, yet he must exert all his powers to prevail and survive with dignity. Faulkner's philosophy in this book has been compared to the theme of Albert Camus' *Myth of Sisyphus*.

The Fable (1954) is a modern version of Christ's life and crucifixion. Its Christ is a French corporal, a simple, uneducated man, during World War One. The corporal has twelve men, corresponding to the twelve apostles, and he is betrayed by one of them, a twentieth-century Judas, and is executed. This parable does not imply that Faulkner accepted the divinity of Christ or that he was a Christian in the conventional sense. In all likelihood he wanted this book to be a fictional corollary of his Nobel prize acceptance speech, in which he declared that man would prevail because "he has a soul, a spirit, capable of compassion and sacrifice and endurance." But much of the critical reaction to this allegorical work was unfavorable. The reviewers said the author did not succeed in making his protagonist a credible, flesh-and-blood figure.

The Town and *The Mansion,* published in 1957 and in 1959 respectively, comprise the second and third parts of the Snopes trilogy, started in *The Hamlet.* But the older Faulkner did not see the moral dilemma between the upstart Flem Snopes and the representatives of the old order as a clear-cut choice between evil and good. *The Town,* which portrays Flem as he is ascending in the social hierarchy after his move to the county seat of Jefferson, conceives of human character in greater complexity than *The Hamlet.* Snopes himself, he appears to say, is in the same boat with the rest of us. He, too, is a victim.

The Mansion further stresses that the Snopeses are caught in the same predicament as the rest of mankind and elicits a comprehensive compassion for all men, including murderers and thieves. Through the multiple-narrator method to which Faulkner returned in these two novels, we are for part of the time introduced into the mind of Mink Snopes, Flem's cousin. Mink has spent thirty-eight years in prison for the murder of Houston. The author brings the reader around to condone and even approve of Mink's action. Mink was a poor tenant farmer who worked hard all through his life until he realized that no matter how much he endured and how much he tried, the economic system would never allow him to lift himself out of his miserable plight, and that his children would inherit his cares and frustrations. He called the forces that worked against him, the men who would always enjoy the fruits of his labors, "they." Houston was an embodiment of this "they" or "them" and Mink regarded his murder not as a crime but a moral imperative. But he survived thirty-eight years of prison only with the thought of committing another murder, killing his cousin Flem Snopes for failing to help him at the time of the trial, though he was then already becoming an influential citizen. On the other hand, we see that Flem himself is not to be envied either. His great frustration in life has been that he is impotent. By cheating and defrauding the community, he was trying to prove that he was as much of a man as the next fellow. Faulkner's reaction to Snopes' impairment is not one of glee but compassion, and instead of a shortcoming, Flem's impotence is presented as the one element in him that admits him to the human race, for it is his Achilles' heel, and the explanation of the evil he has wrought.

The Reivers (1962) is a work in a minor key, the most optimistic and cheerful Faulkner ever wrote. Its protagonist, Lucius Priest, is a sensitive, intelligent and blameless eleven-year-old boy, resembling other sensitive youngsters, largely autobiographical or romanticized-autobiographical, in Faulkner's *oeuvre,* but he is not burdened with the bad conscience or high-strung emotivity of some of the others. The boy and two of his cronies, Boon Hogganbeck, and Ben, a Negro, take off on a jaunt to Memphis in the car that belongs to Lucius' grandfather. Boon wants to pay a visit to Corrie, a prostitute.

In Memphis, Ben swaps the car for a race horse. After a series of amusing incidents they win the car back and return to Jefferson. Corrie has been so impressed by Lucius' innocent charm that she decides to marry Boon and at the end of the book she is showing her infant to Lucius. It is all like a Paul Gallico novel, at times cute but thoroughly unreal. It would be futile to speculate on Faulkner's changed intellectual perspective in this work, which was apparently written with the sole aim of providing entertainment.

DEATH: In 1953, Faulkner's daughter Jill went to study at the University of Mexico in Mexico City and Mrs. Faulkner accompanied her. He spent more and more time away from Oxford. In 1955 he went to Japan on a lecture tour. He visited Europe several times. In 1957 and 1958 he was writer-in-residence at the University of Virginia at Charlottesville. Perhaps he accepted the grant to be near his daughter, for Jill had married and had gone to live in Charlottesville with her husband, Mr. Paul Summers. The record that has been published of the class conferences he held at the university is not without interest, but should not be taken as Faulkner's definitive word on his own production. For one thing, he did not reread his books before the discussions, recalled their plots hazily, and occasionally even confused their characters. Some questions he dodged, to others he gave factually incorrect answers which the students were apparently too embarrassed to point out or pursue.

Photographs taken after 1960 suddenly show the author as an old man. He looks haggard, diminished in stature. But he still gave many lectures. He returned from such an engagement to Oxford in June, 1962. On the morning of July 6th he died of a heart attack.

CRITICAL APPRAISAL: In the early 1930's Faulkner was greeted as a great discovery. His was a new accent in American letters. The themes he treated were of universal significance, but his books also had a regional flavor that appeared fresh and authentic. He was a bit of a noble savage whom the northern literary establishment expected to tame for its purposes. Yet later on the very qualities that helped him emerge from anonymity turned against him. When in the mid-thirties the critics took another look they found him illogical, uncouth, long-winded, and redundant. His technique of withheld meaning, his involved and unclear sentence structure where the reader must hunt for the pronoun reference, his violations of syntax and obscure meaning came in for a re-examination. In a social context, he was accused of having a reactionary message, or of suggesting no solutions at all.

However, academic criticism was beginning to take him into account as a phenomenon worthy of note. During the war years he produced little, yet by the late forties it was found that he had become in the eyes of the young an eminent and revered figure, somewhat out of the past, but a model for imitation and an object of nostalgia. After the Nobel prize it was more difficult to attack him. He was now the grand old man of American literature. His international reputation was immense. Particularly in France he became the idol of a new generation of writers.

Critics who have been concerned with drawing up a balance sheet since his death emphasize the vast range and scope of characters that he created, his great powers of inventiveness. His experiments with structure, with the point of view, are recognized to attest to his versatility. He is sometimes referred to as a regional writer, in the best sense of the word, for he explored in depth the consciousness and human reality of a limited geographical area. He took folk rhetoric as a tool and made it into a vehicle of literary expression.

2. THE SIGNIFICANCE OF *LIGHT IN AUGUST*

Seen in the context of the development of Western literature in the twentieth century, *Light in August* comprises a particular subdivision of the themes of lost identity and search for identity. This subject was introduced by the Romantic school and has gained increasing momentum and importance in our fast-changing culture, where the alienation of urban masses, the vast progress of technology, the threats posed against the individual by standardization, and many other factors, too numerous to name here, have contributed to a sense of vaporization and disappearance of the self.

IDENTITY: *Light in August* is a regional formulation of the problem of disappearing identity. Its protagonist, Joe Christmas, does not know what he is. But the reason for his uncertainty is not metaphysical, epistemological, or even economic. His problem is a racial one. He goes through his life suspecting that he has Negro blood. He does not look like a Negro—he is sometimes called a "wop" by people who do not like him—he has a skin that the author describes as "parchment-colored." At the time he is arrested one of the bystanders remarks, "He looks no more like a nigger than you or I." But his grandfather, a white supremacist, suspects that his daughter's Mexican lover is part Negro, kills the man, and abandons their "tainted" child on the doorstep of an orphanage.

The matron who finds the baby knows nothing of his parentage. Because it is Christmas Eve, she names the boy Joe Christmas. But Doc Hines, Joe's grandfather, is drawn by a secret force to the proximity of his grandchild, whom he considers to be a sign of his sin. He takes a job as janitor at the orphanage. Perhaps because of casual remarks the old man makes, perhaps because of his illegitimacy that they inferred from the fact that he was a foundling, or because of the child's submissiveness due to the malevolent attention that the old man pays to him, or because of his dark complexion, the children call him "nigger." But the most scathing experience takes place when he becomes the unwitting witness of a young woman's sexual promiscuity and is referred to, at the age of five, as an illegitimate Negro.

These words, this phrase, put their stamp on Christmas, and the rest of his life is an attempt to find his place and, when he sees that this is impossible, to avenge himself on society. In the South where Faulkner grew up, the greatest division between men was not created by education, money, religion, occupation, or cultural interests, but by race. For those of us who regard a man's actions as the criterion of his worth this does not make sense. But "black" and "white" belonged to the definition of a person for a Southerner just as much as "intelligent" or "two-legged" do to us. If Joe Christmas ignored whether he was white or Negro, within the context of his peculiar culture, this meant that he did not know what he was, or even whether he was human, for Negroes were hardly thought to be human by those who formulated the standards of the community.

IDENTITY IN RACIAL TERMS: We should not, therefore, be surprised to find that the question of identity is posed in racial terms. The cultural milieu lacked the sophistication, the democratic freedom, the intellectual leisure, as it were, to probe deeper, to see things in a wider perspective, to be able to realize that identity is not a racial but a universally human problem. For Joe Christmas, this was the crucial existential issue. And so it was for Faulkner, who witnessed the fate of Joe Christmases in the stifling atmosphere of his native land.

To be white meant to have one's basic admission to the human race. One could go to a restaurant, provided one had the money. To be black, on the other hand, though it entailed many disadvantages, was still to be part of a large group, as numerous as the white community, within which security could be obtained, where the Negro could move with familiarity, which observed its own mores. But Christmas could not find his place in either camp.

Christmas tried to live among Negroes. But his early training as a white got the better of him. He had been brought up to despise their ways, to look at them with contempt, to dislike even the odor their bodies emanated. The Negroes themselves did not accept him as one of them. He had the appearance of a white man. They nudged him out every time he attempted to join them. They did it more gently than the civilized whites, but he realized that he made them feel uncomfortable. They did not claim him.

When he was among whites, Christmas always knew that he held a secret that, once discovered, would make his friends, his mistresses, his foster parents reject him. He remembered the mysterious old man of his childhood, the other boys who called him a nigger at the orphanage, the dietician who told him he was an illegitimate Negro. He was a fake white. At best he could feel as an enemy, a spy planted among them, and exult over the fact that they were too dumb to find him out. With gleeful malice he would tell white women after they slept with him that he was a Negro. But this was a perverse joy, born of wounds that never healed, of frustration, of hatred.

ACCEPTANCE: His suspicions were never substantiated. Faulkner made it clear that no one knew for certain. As we have said, Christmas "looked like a white man." This, for all practical purposes, signifies that he *was* one. Christmas' illness was of the mind. It had no biological basis. Had he chosen to forget about his suspected ancestry, he could have easily settled down in the village where his adoptive parents lived. His name was now McEachern; no one there was acquainted with his grandfather, now becoming senile, or the dietician. His secret was safe, and he was accepted as a *bona fide* member of the community. But he could not forget about his humiliations in his early childhood. He could not forgive the whites, or himself. He never regarded the McEacherns as his own people. When he was eighteen, Joe thought defiantly of McEachern as a fool who had nursed a nigger beneath his own roof.

INTELLECTUAL HONESTY: Joe Christmas' illness was intellectual honesty. He was his own victim, his own executioner. Like most of Faulkner's tragic characters, he is the captive of his past that he cannot, *would* not disown. This is perhaps a mistake, but one that in Faulkner's eyes commands respect and compassion. The other two tragic figures in the novel, Joanna Burden and Gail Hightower, suffer from the same disease. The Reverend Hightower cannot free himself from his childhood infatuation with the Civil War and the exploits of his legendary grandfather. All his life becomes the reliving of the moment of his grandfather's death. Unlike Christmas, Hightower is a willing victim: he wants to get away from reality. Joanna Burden has sacrificed herself for an ideal that has been instilled in her by her father: one must work to raise the Negroes, who are the white man's shadow, God's curse on the whites.

Joe and Joanna could be each other's salvation—a limited degree of salvation, but one that would make life bearable to each. Joanna Burden sees the Negro in Christmas, the race for whom she has been working. The frustration of her womanhood could be lifted by the very person that belongs to the people who are dear to God because they have had to suffer so much. On the other hand, Joanna is the only woman Christmas ever met who regards his suspected Negro blood as something precious and holy. But here another factor enters into play: religion. Joanna's puritanical faith cannot accept sex outside marriage. She tries to force him to repent what she considers to be their sins. She wants him to pray together with her. And here her behavior causes a short circuit in Joe's consciousness. She calls to his mind McEachern's morality, the atmosphere of his foster parents' home, which he cannot bear. Joanna is getting old. She has the masculinity of a middle-aged woman who has strict principles. She has reached the age of the menopause. She cannot satisfy him, she can only torture him with a religious code that to him is associated with the lies of the white community. They have both reached the end of the road. And now they become each other's hangmen.

CHRIST FIGURE: In the end, Joe lets himself be caught. He is a Christ figure, in that the whites can project into him their own vices and crimes, and he becomes the receptacle of their ordure. As a white Negro, he helps them get rid of the black part of their persons, he pays for their sins, and the participants of the miracle play can go home feeling cleansed. The phony white, who was really a Negro, has been destroyed, the evil part of themselves has been annihilated. Joe did not offer himself up for the redemption of humanity. His act was born of defiance, it was a gesture, a challenge thrown into the face of his civilization. As such, it had no immediate good result. But ultimately, in Faulkner's hands, he has become a weapon fighting prejudice and cruelty. And in this sense he can truly be said to be a vehicle of salvation.

STRUCTURAL ANALYSIS OF *LIGHT IN AUGUST*

SOME INTRODUCTORY COMMENTS: The fact that Lena Grove has come from Doane's Mill, Alabama, is one which Faulkner stresses to introduce us to one of the central themes of the novel namely the conflict between urban and rural civilizations. Faulkner almost invariably prefers the latter, since technological progress has obliterated the integration of pristine communities with nature, and he hammers home this theory by implying that Lena's pregnancy and vagrancy are the outcome of what the sawmill represents. There is also an animal naturalness and innocence about Lena which raises her to the symbolic stature of an ancient fertility goddess, highlighted by her open search for Lucas Burch, the mill-worker responsible for her pregnancy. This search, coupled with her telling of the story to the Armstids, who take her in, point to the pagan quality about Lena's acceptance of joy and pain. Her quality already implies the naturalness of pre-Judaic-Christian civilizations, a theme inherent in the very title of the book, which alludes to antiquity. Faulkner himself was careful to point out that *Light in August* refers to the few August days in Mississippi when there is a haunting quality in the atmosphere which is a premonition of fall.

This light is cast symbolically on earlier cultures, revealing the gods, fauns, and satyrs of ancient Greece, for example. It falls on an age when there was no concept of original sin, and when an innocent acceptance of kindness was a norm. Faulkner implies this by Lena's acceptance of the money offered by Mr. Armstid before she proceeds on the last part of her journey to Jefferson, where she thinks she will find Lucas Burch. At this point, too, the author suggests that Lena's primitive quality makes her universally attractive, as shown by her unshakable confidence that she will find the man who seduced her. In her mind, her right to this man is as natural as it is ancient and inalienable. Note how cleverly Faulkner introduces the reader to themes and characters in advance, by providing data which will be of great significance in future chapters. When Lena is being taken to Jefferson, for example, the yellow column of smoke comes from the burning house of Joanna Burden, who is to be a main character in the novel. This technique of giving advance warning of themes and characters is not unique to Faulkner, but is one that had been used earlier, particularly by the French Romantics, Victor Hugo and Eugene Sue to mention two. Faulkner employs it in his own characteristic way, however, and does not use it merely to heighten suspense. With him it is used on a higher level, and implies a more profound ultimate meaning. When Lena is told, for example, that the man who works in the Jefferson mill is called Bunch, not Burch, not only is our curiosity aroused, but the theme of primitiveness mentioned earlier is again stressed by the girl's reaction. Her faith that Lucas Burch will also be there indicates the pristine innocence which Faulkner found so appealing.

The images of the opening chapter of the novel are worthy of note as well, for in the dust and heat, the clatter of the wagons, and the colors we have some of the mysterious sources of strength which permeate Faulkner's novels. We know at once that we are dealing with the earth and its people. It was this sense of local color that Albert Camus found so appealing in Southern writers. There is also a sense of isolation in the portrayal of Lena Grove, but it is an isolation coupled with a natural dignity and fertile hope. Faulkner is very careful to establish the setting immediately, and to preface the central action with enough information to whet the appetite and lend a grandeur of tone to the novel.

INTRODUCTION TO CHARACTERS: We have seen how Faulkner forecasts characters and events in a unique way. We now find another device he uses to heighten dramatic effect, namely that of the flash back, and he uses a Jefferson millworker, Byron Bunch, to reminisce over a three year period. This sets the whole Jefferson scene to prepare us for Lena's arrival, and gives us an oblique yet penetrating insight into three of the novel's most important characters—Joe Christmas, Joe Brown, and Joanna Burden. The very name "Joe Christmas" intrigues us, as does the manner, attitude, and dress on his arrival in Jefferson. An antithesis to Lena is immediately set up: Christmas, a swarthy man with a contemptuous attitude, seems to have no identity. He is rootless, living between two worlds, a fact which is made clear to us by his being given a menial mill job usually reserved for Negroes, and by his wearing of city clothes. His story arouses our interest, and establishes some symbolism contrary to that evoked by Lena. He represents urban society, but is apparently a victim of civilization rather than one of its exploiters. The fact that he refused Byron Bunch's offer of food and that he was living in a Negro cabin on Miss Burden's estate immediately suggests a mysterious background, while there is something symbolic in his fellow workers' suspicious view of him as being a foreigner.

The arrival of another strange character, Joe Brown, is cleverly depicted by Faulkner to add to the air of anticipation already created. For example, while the name "Joe Brown" is a common one, its very commonness seems as mysterious in context as the name "Joe Christmas." The collusion between Christmas and Brown is interesting too. When they start going out together on Saturdays, for example, we know that something unusual is afoot, since Christmas' withdrawn attitude and Brown's shiftiness do not seem to make for a healthy friendship. The way in which we are told of Christmas' bootlegging business and Brown's joining him after Christmas quit his mill job is also a clever device used by Faulkner to introduce us to Joanna Burden, on whose grounds Christmas and Brown share a cabin.

Joanna's family background supplies one of Faulkner's commentaries on an aspect of Southern society which fits into the general pattern of his theme. The fact that the middle-aged spinster's grandfather had moved south from New Hampshire during the reconstruction era, and that he and her brother had been killed by a former slave-owner, makes Joanna also a victim of history in a sense. In this section we also have another antithetical character in Byron Bunch himself, for ostensibly he does not have the aura of romance, dissolution, mystery or intrigue which surround the other characters. His life is organized, he has abandoned sentimental notions of love, and leads a respectable existence marked by hard work and routine.

It is interesting to note how Faulkner quietly slips back into present action and intensifies the drama by the confrontation between Bunch and Lena. Note how deftly Faulkner shows us that Bunch's air of efficiency is a mask behind which romantic notions *do* in fact lurk. For by the end of the passage in which we learn that Joe Brown is really Lucas Burch—Lena's seducer—and that her knowledge of Burch's changed name and bootlegging operations does not alter her attitude to him, we also learn that Byron Bunch is in love with Lena. Yet note how obliquely Faulkner does this, since he makes the reader aware of Bunch's stirred emotions while making sure that Bunch himself is unaware that his attitude is being torn down by Lena's innocence and charm.

THEMES SUGGESTED BY HIGHTOWER'S CHARACTER: Faulkner's use of the flash back device is masterly in Byron Bunch's recounting the story of Jefferson's former Presbyterian minister, the Reverend Gail Hightower. The fact that Bunch is now Hightower's sole—and secret—friend indicates the theme of loneliness. The portrait of the lonely man waiting for dusk to obliterate the realities of life is a moving and evocative one. We have the feeling that in such a twilight, past glories are relived in a kind of fantasy world of daydreams, and this feeling is reinforced when we learn Hightower's story.

Faulkner is really commenting here on certain uniquely Southern attitudes, as in the minister's attitude to the town of Jefferson when he had arrived there with his wife twenty-five years before, full of romantic dreams of his grandfather's Civil War exploits. The hostility of the townsfolk toward him, together with his wife's gradual decline, infidelity and death, go to highlight Faulkner's theme of death through refusal to love, and social ostracization through avoidance of reality. Faulkner is here attacking not only Hightower for his attitude to his wife—an attitude which led to her death—but also the whole attitude of romanticizing the past and ignoring the present. Note also the fierce symbolism of the scene, after his wife's death, in which Hightower shields his face from photographers by holding the book of Holy Scriptures in front of it—for not only is he shutting out reality, but is also concealing an ironic smile. This near-satanic grin could be interpreted to mean, quite simply, that Hightower is the personification of evil. What Faulkner is really telling us, however, is that Hightower's attitude to his wife's death and the hostility of his congregation represents the attitude of the romantic man toward the mad order of the universe which he cannot comprehend or come to terms with. He is the type of man for whom the only reality lies in the magic fantasy of the past.

The attitude of the local inhabitants toward the disgraced minister does not escape Faulkner's criticism either, however. The gossip centered around the Negro woman who cooked for him after his resignation, and the whipping of his Negro servant by the Klu Klux Klan, do not speak highly of the townspeople's interpretation of Christian charity. Faulkner also meant something deeper. For by their attitude, the people are really projecting the evil of their own character onto him, and displaying their own inability to cope with a man of his undeniable sensitivity. Their argument that Hightower's strange conduct is motivated by another woman in his life, suggests to Faulkner that their own conduct is motivated by petty jealousy.

The final commentary on the whole Hightower background comes with the incident in which the minister, in an act of humane charity, delivers the stillborn Negro baby. The townsfolk's gossip that he was its father and had allowed it to die, and Hightower's reply that he could not blame them for their erroneous belief, constitute a synthesis of Faulkner's private convictions. For many things happen in life, and many attitudes are adopted, for which the individual bears no responsibility, inasmuch as the author of the petty-minded drama in which people have roles is often some traditional, inscrutable being—perhaps just the crazed order of the world. Hightower's words in this instance are important in demonstrating the determinism which became part of Faulkner's literary growth. It is not clearly defined yet, or fully developed by any means in *Light in August,* but there is more than a strong hint of its presence. In the final analysis, the people of Jefferson behave as they have been taught by their parents, and Hightower himself is a victim of a highly romanticized heritage based on fantasy rather than reality. In a very real sense, then, Hightower and the townsfolk can be censured for their conduct on one level or perception, but cannot really be blamed when examined on a wider level.

CHRISTMAS AND THE WHITE NEGRO THEME: This strange and moving theme is introduced to us when Faulkner again slips back into present action. It is fascinating to study the way Faulkner brings us to the idea of Christmas having Negro blood in him. By having Byron Bunch come to tell the Reverend Hightower about Lena's search for Burch, and how he (Byron) had tried to find Burch (Joe Brown) for her, Faulkner is first of all letting us know that Bunch is the only close friend Hightower has—and *vice versa.* Also, when Byron finds out that Christmas and Brown are implicated in the burning of the Burden home, his taking Lena to his own landlady suggests his true feelings toward Lena. Faulkner cleverly uses the murder of Miss Burden to reveal Brown's character and also to disclose the deep-rooted antipathy toward the Negro in Southern society.

The author is careful in his scene-setting at this point. Note how no one takes Brown seriously when he says that Christmas is the murderer and had been Miss Burden's lover for years. The suggestion here is, of course, that the general opinion of

Brown is so low that nothing he says is believed—until he claims that Christmas has Negro blood in him. This is quite a brilliant piece of incisive writing on Faulkner's part, for the interrogating marshal's sudden change of attitude toward Brown when he hears this, encompasses the whole tradition of prejudice against the Negro. Yet it is interesting to note how even Brown is reluctant to reveal the information, and it is implied that Christmas' Negro blood is his last desperate attempt to save his own skin.

Faulkner here reveals a tremendous amount by implication, for everything Brown says seems to make sense within the context of an atmosphere riddled with racial prejudice. A very subtle psychological and racial situation is now suggested to us. The white people of Jefferson have been conditioned, of course, to regard Negroes as being automatically guilty. But we have the hint here that somewhere deep inside the white community there is a feeling that the Negro is not the only one who harbors evil thoughts and perpetrates foul deeds.

Faulkner is now in the area of white guilt, and Brown's revelation about Christmas' Negro blood—whether the accusation is true or false does not matter to the white Jefferson mentality—comes along as a kind of *deus ex machina.* For while it has been the time-honored custom to shovel all the garbage of accusations onto the Negro's heap, this has never solved the white man's problem of how to empty his guilt regarding the Negro. What the townsfolk did to Hightower did not solve the problem, since he was a white man, and their traditional treatment of the Negro has merely added fuel to their own hate and guilt. The ideal victim therefore, would be a white Negro—by that Faulkner does not mean necessarily a white man who has Negro blood in him, but a white man who is also a Negro.

Such a person may seem a myth or a symbol, but Faulkner is telling us that he is a very real being who lurks within each one of us. When Brown reveals this about Christmas, he is therefore giving the white population the opportunity to lynch not only a murderer, but to murder the guilt within itself and to expose and destroy the Negro part of its being vicariously and cathartically. Faulkner does all this brilliantly by implication, of course, for the sheriff immediately responds to Brown as a brother. Faulkner, in so doing, opens up new dimensions to the novel. But he also arouses our interest in Christmas, and makes us wonder about his real nature, his background, and makes us wish to examine his new role as a white Negro.

THE IDENTITY AND PERSONALITY OF CHRISTMAS: Faulkner's structural technique is masterful in the next section, for by relating what happens in the present, he covers the time immediately preceding Miss Burden's murder, and is still able to delve deeply into Christmas' past to give us some clues to his personality and behavior patterns. The scene in which the drunken Brown calls Christmas a Negro not only reveals the fact that he is a worthless person, but shows up the Christmas-Brown relationship in a new light. For we can see Christmas as a Christ figure without a mission and with no redemption to offer. His only disciple is Brown, who, throughout all his empty chatter and witticisms, admired Christmas for his silence, energy and will-power. But his sole disciple is a Judas, who betrays his master by baring to him—and to the reader—the raw wounds of Christmas' inner dichotomy.

Christmas is yet a more tragic figure than Christ, because he not only loses his only disciple, but realizes finally that he does not belong in any world. Notice, for example, that during the day before the murder he sees some white people in a car, and he curses them, although they do not hear him; later he passes some Negroes, who call him a white man. His wrath at both sections of the community leaves him in an ethnic vacuum. He regards the whites as accursed aliens to be envied, and the Negroes as despised trash of whom he is jealous for their attitude to him of self-assertion, an attitude they display with neither haughtiness nor humility, infuriating him. He has therefore become a man with no identity and no one with whom to communicate; he is utterly alone, and this makes his condition more tragic. His decision to commit murder is the outcome of this unbearable tension, but even the murder assumes wider dimensions than one would normally suppose.

The murder will be a token of revolt, of course, a gesture of rebellion against the world into which Christmas has been hurled and in which he has no place. The important thing to note is *who* is to be the victim. Christmas does not even contemplate killing some symbol of authority, such as a policeman or a public official, so his rebellion is not purely of a social nature. The victim will not be Brown, who is now a totally meaningless figure to him. The fact that Christmas chooses to kill a middle-aged woman seems to indicate that she must represent the strange forces in his background which made him what he is—a white Negro.

Faulkner now shows how influenced he was by Freud's doctrines, which stressed the importance of traumatic childhood sex experiences in developing the individual. In order to lay bare the inner dynamism which motivates Christmas, he regresses in time once more and helps us solve the enigma of Joe's personality. His experiences in the orphanage as a young child of discovering the dietician and the intern having intercourse, of eating the toothpaste through fright at the discovery, and at being called an illegitimate Negro by the dietician, give us two important psychogenetic factors. Because he was consuming the sticky, nauseatingly sweet toothpaste while watching the sex act, sex will always have repulsive connotations for him. Secondly, when the dietician brands him as a Negro, this has a deep-rooted effect on him, since she represents the adult world, and therefore her pronouncement has the ring of authority about it. The dietician's fear at the possibility of the boy's revealing what he had seen, his rejection of her attempted bribery, and her approaching the janitor of the orphange, all help to fill in his background. The fact that the child was found abandoned at Christmas, for example, not only explains his name, but also gives further backing to the Christ analogy. Note throughout all this how Faulkner moves unobtrusively from the present into the past and back again.

CHRISTMAS' CHILDHOOD AND BACKGROUND: When the dietician approaches the janitor, she shows a remarkable degree of intuition, and through their conversation Faulkner reveals more of Christmas' psychology. The fact that the other children in the orphanage refer to Christmas as a Negro—which the dietician had used against him—probably arose from his having dark skin and from the hateful looks which the boy received from the old janitor. Faulkner finally takes us to the root of Joe's psyche by exposing the fact that the old man, who removes the boy from the orphanage, is his grandfather. We now have the primary awareness that harks back to his earliest reminiscences, and the basis of his consciousness is that he is different. Even his own grandfather thinks he has Negro blood in him, and the boy therefore regards the old man as a kind of malevolent deity looking down upon him.

The next stage in Christmas' development was his adoption

by a puritanical, God-fearing man called McEachern. The boy's opposition to his foster parent in refusing to memorize a part of the catechism constituted, for Faulkner, the day on which Christmas became a man. Manhood for Faulkner meant the assertion of one's will, and the boy's negative assertion was probably a token of his disowning a civilization that had already destined him to be a pariah. We know from the boy's attitude to McEachern that his sense of "otherness" had been already deeply engrained in his character, since his foster parent does not suspect his being part Negro.

The fact that the whipping which McEachern administered was almost relished by the boy, also suggests deep-rooted disturbances which come out later when he starts to kick a Negro girl with whom he has had intercourse. Again the beating he receives from McEachern is received with an attitude akin to ecstasy. His behavior with the girl can be traced back to his witnessing the sexual act between the dietician and the intern. Disgusted and humiliated then, his reaction to having sexual intercourse is a violent one, particularly since the girl is a Negro, with whom he feels a sense of identification. The joy with which he receives the whippings also recalls the attitude of mediaeval monks toward self-flagellation.

His relationship with Bobbie, the waitress, is a touching one, and for a time he seems to have overcome his disgust with sex and combined physical and emotional love in his feelings for her. This is achieved despite his horror at discovering what menstruation is. It is interesting to note that he cleansed himself symbolically of his horror by killing a sheep. Faulkner makes the break-up with Bobbie dramatic, but although it involves physical violence with McEachern, the tremendous blow to Joe was not the fact that she was a prostitute, but that she had flung the old accusation in his face: he was a Negro.

During the years of wandering that followed, his reaction to what women thought of him when he said he was a Negro is interesting. His apparent indifference to a contemptuous attitude contrasts strangely with his violent reaction when women said it made no difference. What he was really doing was not trying to be loved, but to shock them. When a woman showed indifference to his "color" however, the white part of his thinking and background come out in the form of violence. In many ways he had adopted ethnically the attitude which his foster parent had shown morally. To McEachern, it was morally justifiable for him to go to a brothel, but it was sinful for Joe. To Joe, a white man may have a Negro mistress, but it was unthinkable for a white woman to give herself to a Negro. His own ethnic duality added to the pangs of alienation he was already suffering.

CHRISTMAS AND JOANNA: Christmas' fifteen years of wandering constituted an odyssey to escape from himself, and his encounter with Miss Burden has great symbolic significance. Because of her background, her anti-segregationist views do not imply that she believes in equality. Negroes to her are a God-given curse, and she believed that it is our duty to raise their standards, although equality can never be achieved. Their sexual affair created a struggle within her between passion and the uncompromising demands of religion, one of Faulkner's recurring themes. The result is violence, hypocrisy, and casting around for a scapegoat when the suspected evil is actually within us. It results in lynchings, in the dismissal of the Reverend Hightower's cook, and in McEachern's whipping his own sins out of his foster child. In Joanna's case it ends in a double personality. There will be a clash of the New England glacier and the Protestant hell, and Joanna's murder by Christmas is the result. The fact that she had suggested his going to a Negro school constituted an unbearable humiliation for Joe. We must remember his dual attitude here, for he had lived with Negroes before and was in the habit of daring them to say he was white.

Faulkner has been criticised for the violence of the scene in which Joe slaps Joanna prior to the murder, since the scene seems somewhat contrived. The best explanation for it is that Christmas could call himself a Negro if he wished, but that he would not allow anyone to *tell* him. We must bear in mind too the deep scars left on his personality because of his first encounter with sex and the duality of his mental attitude toward himself as a white Negro. A whole combination of factors leads to his choice of Joanna as the victim of his pent up emotions.

CHRISTMAS, HINES, AND HIGHTOWER: The Christ parallel comes up again in Christmas' putting up no resistance to being captured—in this case, he had nothing to hope for from life. Faulkner has again been criticised for introducing Hines, an old man who turns out to be Christmas' grandfather, the former janitor of the orphange. Although it seems too much of a coincidence that the old man is living in the town where Christmas is arrested, Faulkner probably introduces him to show how deep-rooted prejudice can be. There is also the psychological factor to consider, since Hines is a small man who, having been mocked so often for his size, has to find someone to look down on. The Negro in general is the obvious target, and Christmas in particular comes in for his contempt because of the blood tie involved. Yet it is interesting to note that Faulkner does not make Hines an object of contempt himself, and here we have Faulkner's deterministic theory coming into play again.

The Reverend Hightower is reintroduced here, probably as some kind of commentary on his Christian position. His concern has been the fear of what will happen to Joe if he is caught, yet when Bunch suggests that he save Christmas by saying that it was *he* who had been having the affair with Christmas, he refuses. His successful delivery of Lena Grove's baby, and his persuading Bunch not to try to marry Lena constitute a highpoint in his life. For a brief moment he is happy, but there is no permanent solution for him. He is a lost man, condemned to loneliness because of the past. It seems that happiness is reserved for people like Lena who live in the present and accept life without an afterthought.

The final scene in which Joe strikes Hightower, but does not kill him is interesting. Joe's Negro mind took him to a Negro cabin to get the pistol to kill Hightower, but his white mind made it impossible for him to kill the man. There is therefore no salvation for Christmas, except by being killed himself. There is even a hideous symbolism in his death, since the man who shot him and emasculates him while he is still living is called Grimm.

CHRISTMAS, RELIGION AND DEATH: There was no way out of Christmas' murdering of Joanna Burden. The fact is that he had tried to act as a white man and as a Negro, but could perform neither role successfully. The only thing he could expect from her after fifteen years of wandering was security, but the deep-rooted problems proved insoluble. Joanna to him was Woman, the cause of man's fall, repulsive, tantalizing, mysterious, and nauseating. She was white and, because of Joe's Negro mentality, superior. Even her cooking reminds Joe of McEachern's stern moral postures. Note that from the very beginning it was the catechism that Joe refused to learn, since this was a moral code which in fact had made a pariah of him. Religion to Christmas was a white man's religion, and when Joanna exhorted him to pray he identified her with the forbidding foster father. So when Joe murders Joanna, he is killing his foster father and Womanhood all in one. Had there been any way out of it, any faint glimmer of hope, he would have left her.

In a way Christmas had reached a spiritual impasse, and there was no escape. He had to do something symbolically drastic, he had to make a final, agonizing gesture of protest as an eternal monument to his life. He knew and did not really care that he would be killed as a result. He is an innocent victim, and in this way again, he is a Christ figure. He consented to die because all hope was abandoned, however, and because there was no salvation—in this way he is the antithesis of Christ.

HIGHTOWER, LENA, AND THE END: Faulkner makes great use of symbolism at the end of the book by having the Reverend Hightower alone in his study at dusk. He then uses his technique of reminiscing to reveal many aspects about Hightower's past life, and there is a bitterly grim irony in the fact that the romantic episode of his grandfather's death was ludicrous, since he had been killed in the act of stealing chickens from a coop. Note how the author has kept the circumstances of the grandfather's death to the very end, yet by creating such an ironical anti-climax, Faulkner is not making Hightower a simple fool. There is an autobiographical element here, since through Hightower, Faulkner is looking at his own infatuation for his great-grandfather. Hightower has lived vicariously in a romantic myth surrounding his grandfather, and the choice was a deliberate one, for the minister found reality coarse and unpoetical.

There is also a symbolic aspect to the end of the book, which, like the beginning, shows us Lena traveling. This does not mean that she is the eternal, shiftless wanderer, by any means. Faulkner makes her more the model of tranquility, self-assurance and motherhood. The aimless, rootless wanderer was Joe Christmas, in fact, the symbol of the restless spirit. It is interesting to note that in leaving without Burch (Brown) and in meeting Byron Bunch at the end, a note of hope prevails. The fact that man will prevail is the final mood of the book, as it was the final note in Faulkner's Nobel prize acceptance speech.

CRITICAL COMMENTARY

FAULKNER ON FAULKNER: In this section we shall first examine Faulkner's own interpretation of *Light in August* as given at class conferences at the University of Virginia in 1957–58, when the author was writer-in-residence there. His comments on his literary production are not always enlightening. Nor was Faulkner a man to quibble over details, to be very precise about his themes, or to claim that he knew all the answers. His answers to students were spontaneous, off the cuff. He did not appear to have read the respective novels before class discussion. He prided himself on not being a literary man, and a certain nonchalance about his own works was apparently an expression of his unwillingness to make profound critical statements for all eternity.

Yet the record of these discussions is helpful because in great outline it indicates how Faulkner felt about the basic symbolism of his novels. On the evidence of Faulkner's own words we shall be in a better position to evaluate the relevance and correctness of the Faulkner criticism, though we do not by any means wish to suggest that the author was infallible or necessarily more incisive than some of the critics.

Faulkner had often been attacked, particularly by his early critics, for not respecting the physical time sequence but instead, jumping back and forth, using flash backs and even a succession of flash backs, thus confusing the reader. When, in connection with *Light in August*, he was asked by a student why he put Hightower's early life in the end of the novel, rather than where Hightower appears for the first time, he answered that this was a question of how to arrange the different parts most effectively, in the most advantageous juxtaposition.

Asked whether Joe Christmas had any black blood, Faulkner said that the point was that Christmas did not know. He did not know, and therefore he was nothing. Faulkner added that to his mind this was the most tragic condition a human being could ever find himself in. But, another student objected, an attorney named Gavin Stevens explains Christmas' action in terms of a conflict of blood. The student referred to the part where Stevens asserts that it was Christmas' black blood that made him go to the cabin, it was his white blood that would not let him kill the Reverend Hightower, etc. Faulkner said Gavin's explanation was a mere rationalization. The white community decided what Christmas was, but Christmas did not know. Nevertheless, in all objectivity, in the novel it sounds very much as though the author identified himself with this theory of conflict of blood, even if we admit that Joe himself did not know, nor did Gavin Stevens have any positive evidence.

About the religious convictions that motivate Hines and McEachern in the novel, Faulkner expressed his implicit disapproval by stating that he always preferred a personal to an organized religion.

Faulkner often said that at the point of starting a novel he never knew exactly how he would finish it—that the characters resolved themselves, as it were. It is interesting to learn from him that when he conceived *Light in August* he did not have the problem of identity in mind at all. He was thinking of Lena Grove, that is, of a pregnant young girl searching for her sweetheart.

Talking of the Reverend Hightower, Faulkner's observations were largely negative and not particularly revealing. Hightower destroyed his wife and wrecked his own life, he said. He had only one thing left that was fine and pure, the memory of his galloping grandfather. Branching out into what he had borrowed from the New Testament to write *Light in August* and some of his other novels, Faulkner said that the Bible is part of our heritage, it is our background, and therefore it is useful raw material for a writer, being readily understood by most of the readers. This had nothing to do, he added, with how much he actually believed in the New Testament.

Faulkner said that he did not at all intend to picture in Christmas the universal human predicament. He did not wish to imply that the tragic view of life was the only correct one. Joe Christmas was a tragic person, that is all. He pointed to the figures of Lena Grove and Byron Bunch to exemplify his belief in the basic possibility of happiness and virtue.

One of the students observed that the names in the book are very suggestive, especially Hightower's and Burden's. Faulkner assented, saying that this was in the tradition of the pre-Elizabethans. Talking of Joanna Burden, he made the remark that some of her hostility (*hardness* would be a better word to describe it) may have come from her New England tradition—or, he said, she may have hated herself because she had come to accept, despite her expressed convictions, the belief, so widespread in the South, that the Negro was incapable of change.

Asked whether he had intended any Christ symbolism in *Light in August,* Faulkner said no. He claimed that he had "no deliberate intent" to repeat the Christ story. Yet other parts of Faulkner's answer indicate that he did think of Christ when he was writing about Christmas. Actually, a cue is given in the novel itself, and almost at the beginning, when Byron Bunch says, "a man's name, which is supposed to be just the sound for who he is, can be somehow an augur of what he will do." Why Faulkner should have wished to deny the obvious parallel is something one can only speculate on. Perhaps it was because from a conventional point of view Christmas is an evil character: he is a murderer. In any case, one student seemed to protest against using Christ as a parallel for "such a sort of bad man." But there Faulkner protested energetically. Joe was not a bad man, he said. Joe's only solution was to live outside mankind. This is what he tried to do, Faulkner argued, but mankind would not let him. In fact, though, this was not what Joe Christmas did. He did not lead a solitary life. He did not really repudiate mankind to the extent that he would have been willing to live alone, even to the extent Hightower lived alone. Faulkner does not seem to realize that Joe's problem was totally a social one. Outside of society no one is black or white in the sense that this is used by us. If only one man lived on earth it would make no difference to him whether he was black or white. We use these terms comparatively. If Joe had gone off to a deserted island and lived there as a second Robinson Crusoe, there would have been no race problem for him.

Finally, Faulkner explained the origin of the title of the novel. In the middle of August, when there is a foretaste of fall already in the air, there is a cool luminosity that reminds one of the Greek sky, of mythical times. The title, Faulkner thought, was a reference to Lena who had this pagan quality in her of being able to assume the joys and sufferings of life.

FREDERICK J. HOFFMAN: Professor Frederick J. Hoffman builds his critique of *Light in August* on the premise that the novels dialectic is the duality of the race problem and of Calvinist harshness in Joe Christmas' formation. Hoffman sees Joe violently asserting his identity from the time he leaves McEachern's house. We do not think that this is a correct appraisal of what is happening to Joe. He is violent, but he is so just because he has *not* found himself. He has not anything to assert, in the way of identity. Joe's problem is not that he has no personality in the sense this is generally meant by modern novelists. He is not in doubt about his metaphysical or epistemological foundations. Objectively, his problem is psychological. But he thinks that it is the biological composition of his body that is at stake.

Professor Hoffman points out that Burden's and Joe's deaths are actually part of one action. Theirs is a double suicide or a double murder. They depended on each other for their lives and for their death. Christmas accepted his own death when he murdered Joanna Burden, and Joanna had reserved the second bullet for herself after she was to have shot Joe.

WILLIAM VAN O'CONNOR: As for Hightower's character, Professor O'Connor in *The Tangled Fire of William Faulkner* expresses the opinion that the minister's refusal to help the jailed Christmas was Faulkner's means of criticizing doctrinal Christianity. To us this inference does not seem to be justified. Hightower does not stand for the church's doctrine. He is a highly unorthodox churchman. He has been removed from the pulpit. Accepting this premise, Professor Hoffman accuses Hightower of denying Christmas his humanity. It is difficult to see how Hightower did this. To refuse to testify publicly that one is a homosexual hardly amounts to a refusal of humanity.

To have done this, Hightower would have had to be a saint—which he admittedly was not. Nor did Joanna Burden refuse to regard Joe as human—as Hoffman apparently believes. In fact, Hightower and Burden were the only two persons who fully accepted Joe as a man despite their awareness that he had, or may have had, Negro blood.

ALFRED KAZIN: Alfred Kazin's illuminating study, "The Stillness of *Light in August*," revolves around the antithesis between Lena Grove and Joe Christmas. He identifies the former with naturalness and the country, and the latter with urban civilization. This is an aspect that we too have emphasized in our analysis of the novel, yet it should be pointed out that it is an exaggeration to say that Joe personifies the city man who "walks all city pavements," Kazin says "with the same isolation and indifference." Joe Christmas is representative of the city in only certain ways. City dwellers are not, as a rule, a mixture of white and Negro. If they are, this is not necessarily their biggest problem, and if it is their biggest problem, it would be so if they lived in the country.

It is equally misleading, in our view, to portray Joe as the principle of "anti-life" or an "abstraction," as Kazin does. To equate Joe with the destructive urban culture which lays waste to the natural beauty of agricultural Mississippi is to forget that Joe is a victim. He never brought about the deforestation of the southern countryside. It is also false to assume that Faulkner sees country mores as bucolic and pastoral in every case. McEachern is an old-fashioned, countrified type. On the other hand, Joe Christmas is not an abstraction either. He has a very definite and strong personality in many ways. There is no question of his will power, of his emotions, of his refusal of his foster parents' moral code. It is only with respect to race that he is ill-defined. He is not "man" trying to discover the particular kind of man he is. Joe is a very special case; his search is not man's search of identity, but an unfortunate, specific, fractional quest for something that is not at the center of the problem.

Kazin claims that, from the moment he appears, Joe Christmas is seen "as what others say about him, he is only a thought in other people's minds." This is another inaccurate statement. It is true that he is tragically wounded and influenced by what others say of him; but there is no doubt that he *is*, he exists with agonizing pain, and he acts all through his life. He is not withdrawn. He is not an introvert. He burns the memory of his existence into the hearts of people, he erects a tombstone for himself in the murder of Joanna Burden.

EDMOND L. VOLPE: Edmond L. Volpe in his study of *Light in August* emphasizes that Joanna and Joe become alter-egos for each other. Perhaps it is more accurate to say that they are each other's complements. Joe is a white Negro—Joanna is a Negro (-loving) white. Joe is an atheist who often acts like a puritan—Joanna is a believer who frequently acts like a heathen. Yet their obsessions are such that they cannot ultimately save each other. Of course, the consideration of Joanna's age, the fact that she is no longer a woman for Christmas, having reached the age of the menopause, is also something that should be considered here, but scholars and critics have had a tendency to overlook this factor, as it does not conveniently fit into any category of symbolic generalization.

CHARLES H. NILON: Charles H. Nilon's *Faulkner and the Negro* exhaustively and incisively examines Joe Christmas' personality and is from this point of view undoubtedly the best study of *Light in August.* His treatment shows a deeper understanding and a firmer grasp of the dynamism that works in Christmas than that of any other critic known to us. He starts out with Richard Chase's statement that "in *Light in August* Faulkner seems to be concerned with showing that the codes modern man *does* set up do *not* allow him to define himself as human—that codes have become compulsive patterns which man clings to in fear and trembling while the pattern emasculates him." Nilon goes on to say that the connotations of "Negro" form the basis of myths whereby whites set their attitudes and that Negroes also conform to at times because the entire system forces them to. "The individual who is Joe Christmas," Nilon observes, "is submerged beneath the social being that a word connotes." In other terms, Christmas is the victim of a monumental hoax that presupposes some magic dividing line between Negroes and whites. Joe's problem is purely a mental one, and it has been inherited from a pre-Civil War ideology. Joe, who has been duped by it, petrifies himself into these supposedly existing attitudes and becomes his own executioner. This, in our opinion, is the clearest and most accurate statement of the evil that gnaws in him: Joe cannot let his real personality emerge, because he is devoured by two mythical creatures, Whiteness and Blackness.

SUMMING UP: Professor Van O'Connor shows that from the point of view of technique *Light in August* skillfully interweaves three different strands, Lena, Hightower, and Christmas-Burden. Lena and Christmas are pitted against each other as two completely contrasting personalities. The Reverend Hightower is also Lena's antithesis—he has many traits that are similar to Christmas. Hightower cannot find himself either, though the reasons for his failure are different. He is afraid of and disgusted by reality. The social role that has been assigned to him is in no way inferior. He is white, a man of the cloth, his financial standards and the respect he is entitled to are above the average in the community. It is not that he is dissatisfied with the role of a minister. He would like no role or situation once he found out their less appealing sides. Hightower's problem *is* a universally human one, because, having overcome or rather never having had to face the handicaps that Joe Christmas started out with, he saw that man's lot is a pitiful one even when he is not scorned because of his race, when he can fill his belly three times a day, and has a roof over his head. The true problem of man's search for identity is seen in Hightower, not Christmas, who can never reach a universal level because of his humiliating struggle to be accepted as a human being at all.

Professor O'Connor rightly underscores, we believe, the lesson that *Light in August* teaches us: men should treat each other charitably and be tolerant of human weaknesses. The violence that is reflected in the novel has been generated by the failure of its characters to love one another.

ESSAY QUESTIONS AND ANSWERS

1. Show all the data in Christmas' life on which the Christ-parallel could be predicated.

ANSWER: His name is Joseph Christmas. The first part of his last name and his initials are the same as Jesus Christ's. He was found on Christmas day. Little is known of him between his childhood and until he is in his early thirties. It has been claimed that Joe's three years with Miss Burden correspond to the three-year period of Christ's mission. Joe's visit to the negro church symbolizes Christ driving the money-lenders out of the temple. His disciple, Joe Brown, to whom he reveals the truth (about himself), betrays him, like Judas, for money. Joe's grandfather thought he was God or the voice of God.

2. Indicate why the Christ-Christmas parallel is paradoxical rather than strictly meant.

ANSWER: Christmas brings no salvation. The immediate result of his execution is the strengthening of prejudice. The townspeople who want to lynch him, Brown and the posse that hunt him down are only actors in a passion play who do not realize the barbarity of what they are doing. They behave as they are expected to by the standards they have been taught, that have been transmitted to them through their fathers and grandfathers. Each has his little part to play. Tragically, Hightower is the only one who sees the senseless and absurd nature of it all. They are puppets, the rest of them, including

Joe Christmas, who has never realized that his dilemma is an imaginary one. Hightower is an impotent man of good will. He has not enough courage to save Joe and he does not wish to involve himself, though it is clear enough to him that Joe is no ordinary criminal. Hightower is a modern Pontius Pilate. He washes his hands.

Moreover, Christ willingly took upon himself the burden of his humanity. Christmas deliberately "ejected himself from the human race," as Faulkner put it. Christ is a symbol of love. Christmas can be defined more in terms of his hatreds, and all his love relationships are aborted, perverted, and unsuccessful. It would therefore be a mistake to talk of *Light in August* as a retelling of the Christ story.

3. How are some of the names descriptive of their bearers in *Light in August?*

ANSWER: We have already discussed the name of Joe Christmas. Joanna Burden: her first name indicates that she is Christmas' complement. Joe and Joanna are means for each other, even though they must also destroy each other. *Burden* symbolizes the fact that she must bear the burden of the white race for its sins. Gail Hightower: he withdraws to his ivory tower, refusing to commit himself, to participate in life. The concept of the ivory tower was a literary convention at the time Faulkner was first exposed to the magic of letters. It was one of the favorite images of decadent poets around the turn of the century. The decadent movement made a lasting impression on Faulkner's fiction, and it is likely that this was his principal association in connection with the minister who is a poet, who has in fact turned his whole life into poetry in order not to be bothered with prosaic details.

4. Can we accept Gavin Stevens' theory that it was a conflict of blood in Joe Christmas that accounts for his contradictory behavior during the last hour of his life?

ANSWER: To answer this with finality and objectively, we should know whether biologically Christmas was part Negro or not. But Faulkner's point in writing about Joe was to have someone about whom it is not known whether his father was just a Mexican of Spanish descent or a mulatto. Moreover, even if we had the proof of his partially Negro ancestry, we would have to establish that there is such a thing as a *biologically* grounded Negro behavior. It seems much more likely that what we associate with Negro conduct is the result of cultural rather than biogenetic factors.

However, were we to ask whether *Faulkner* thought that characteristic Negro attitudes such as he portrayed in his books were the result of the Negro's biological make-up, the answer would probably be yes. It would be to piously whitewash the truth to allege that Faulkner was completely untouched by the Southern white ideology of racial superiority. Northern writers who have tended to do so were probably motivated by the best of intentions, but their interpretations of Faulkner's convictions often make us suspect that they were trying to read their own views into Faulkner's words.

In the 1950's Faulkner became a kind of moderate spokesman for the South. Time and again he emphasized that our relations to the Negroes should be guided by a feeling of compassion, that discrimination was evil, that the white man has committed sins for which he must atone. Yet one cannot escape the impression that his tone was often one of benevolent superiority. With the passing of time, his views came closer and closer to an implied equality, but never seemed to have quite reached that point. A few years before his death he said in an interview that if a conflict were to erupt between the North and South over the racial issue, he would be fighting under the Confederate flag.

5. Characterize Joe Christmas' sexual experiences, pointing out their importance in shaping his personality.

ANSWER: Joe's first encounter with physical love made it seem repulsive to him. It was associated with nausea, with a feeling of guilt, and with his being called an illegitimate Negro. But it is briefly mentioned that he had a more pleasant experience with a girl of about twelve who was affectionately drawn to him as if he had been her child, and when this girl disappeared one day Joe felt a sense of loss, even though he was not very deeply moved.

The polarity between physical love, grasped as repulsive, and affection, judged to be desirable, explain some of Joe's later reactions. The contact with the Negro girl was purely physical. Without quite knowing why he does it, he starts kicking her. When he is told about menstruation, Joe's abhorrence is extreme. He finally shoots a sheep and thereby hopes to have symbolically eliminated the fact of menstruation.

He is attracted to Bobbie by love that is usually referred to as Platonic, spiritual in the sense that it is not connected with the idea of copulation, affectionate rather than physical. That Bobbie wanted to go to bed with him was a surprise to him. But in this case he accepted sex without shock, and now physical and affectionate components were succesfully united in Bobbie as an object of satisfaction. He told Bobbie the secret of his suspected racial background. He hoped to establish a relationship of mutual trust and dependence with the girl. But soon after came disenchantment. Bobbie proved unworthy of his confidence. His picture of salvation was suddenly shattered.

The relationship with Mrs. McEachern can hardly be called sexual, but she represents one aspect of woman to him, and therefore she too should be mentioned here. Mrs. McEachern stands for another part of womanhood that Joe dislikes, not because it is revoltingly anatomical or debasingly physical, though. He is repulsed by her softness, by her inability to assert herself, her hesitancy, and humiliated, apologetically offered affection. He resents her old age, with its bodily infirmity. He regards her and behaves towards her as one would with an old rag. She is the one example through whom Joe's behavior is shown up as thoroughly discreditable and unworthy.

After the conclusion of the adventure with Bobbie, Christmas no longer expects to find a spiritual union with women. Through the waitress his physical desires have been awakened and sex has become an urge and a need for him, but he does not trust white women. He still tells them he is a Negro, but, and this should be remembered, for completely different reasons than he once told it to Bobbie. Now it is a defiance, a vengeance: it is done maliciously.

Thinking that he is not white, that he can approach white women only on a basis of deception, Joe now wants to accept himself as a Negro and takes a Negro mistress. But here he finds that he does not really desire Negresses. Faulkner describes Joe as writhing and straining "with physical outrage and spiritual denial" while he is having sex with the woman who resembles an ebony carving. His early training gets the better of him. This type of sex experience is not the solution.

Having tried and got nowhere all these years, Joe finally meets Joanna Burden who would seem to be the answer to all the misfortunes and disappointments of his life. She is physically white, yet she feels with the Negro. When he first sees her she appears to be a little over thirty, or just about his age. She can accept him as he is, yet she is also desirable. This is a repetition of the relationship with Bobbie, but now perhaps without the bitter awakening at the end.

There is in fact no bitter awakening in the sense that Joanna would be shifty and treacherous like Bobbie. Yet she too has a double personality. At night she is sensual, caressing, passionate; she is the female in love. Her day self is the New England iceberg. Christmas is not concerned with this day self. He does not talk to her during the day. He eats the meals that she has prepared for him in her absence. The catastrophe occurs when the day self intrudes into the night one. At such times Miss Burden assumes a masculine role. She becomes confused with the image of sanctimonious, aggressive McEachern, who used to make Joe pray with him, who used to make him kneel down. Worse still, Joanna's religious period occurs just after it has become evident that she is not expecting, that she has been experiencing the onset of the menopause, which for Christmas denotes that she no longer is a woman.

As we see, McEachern's and Joanna's figures are thus fused semi-consciously for Christmas. The relationship with McEachern was also an equivocally sexual one. Joe used to derive an ecstatic delight from it by looking at his own body as an object, as Faulkner puts it, "a post or a tower upon which the sentiment part of him mused like a hermit," while McEachern was whipping him. This is what we call masochism. Joanna's attitude towards her own body during the time of their successful love relationship is described by Faulkner in the same terms as the child Christmas' attitude towards his body. He speaks of her "rapt and tireless and detached interest" in her physical body. She too derives masochistic pleasure from sexual torture as Christmas once did. As a man, Christmas assumed McEachern's sadistic attitude. He thought that it was his prerogative as a man to defile the bodies of women: he regarded the *other's* body now as the object of pleasure. Miss Burden wanted to reduce Christmas to his former state of childhood submission. But he had almost killed McEachern once when he had just identified himself as an adult and when McEachern tried to deprive him of Bobbie.

Joanna's insistence on prayer caused an emotional short circuit in Joe Christmas. Because he had already found that no other roads were open to him, Christmas decided to kill her in a fashion that also amounted to suicide.

6. Are there any similarities between Joe Christmas and the Reverend Gail Hightower?

ANSWER: Both are in search of identity, both are victims of their past, neither can find fulfillment in sex, both are essentially men of good will who have gone astray.

There is a great deal of autobiographical element in Hightower and Christmas. They both belong to the type of the sensitive Faulknerean hero, though they do not present him in his pristine and original form. Both are wounded by direct contact with life, though Joe later overcomes his revulsions by the exaggerated assertion of his aggressiveness.

Curiously enough, even some of the external data of Joe's and Hightower's lives coincide. On the one hand, we have Hightower's elderly parents with whom the child feels no contact, who are strangers to him, phantoms as he calls them. Mrs. Hightower is weak, sickly, incapable. On the other hand, Christmas' adoptive parents make him feel an outsider. They never understand the child. Mrs. McEachern too is almost an invalid, looks fifteen years older than her age, she too is unsubstantial. Hightower's wife is several years older than the minister, emaciated, on the verge of spinsterhood. Bobbie is described as considerably older than Christmas, she too has sharp features and an emaciated face. The revelation of physical sex is a shock to both, and even the way they express their disappointment is similar.

If Hightower has driven his wife to suicide, Christmas has murdered Joanna. Neither can establish a permanently satisfactory sexual relationship. Both ultimately reject life, Christmas by letting himself be murdered, the Reverend Hightower by identification with his dead grandfather. Hightower's religious convictions or his lack of courage prevent him from literally taking his own life, but he is substantially dead when we see him the last time.

Both Hightower and Christmas are outcasts, which they have chosen to be, not because they essentially liked this condition, but because no other way was open to them whereby they could have still *honestly* functioned as part of the social matrix. And honesty was their prerequisite. They both substantiate the critics' claim that in Faulkner's world the intellectual is invariably faced with a tragic destiny.

BIBLIOGRAPHY

Works by William Faulkner

The Marble Faun (Poems). Boston: The Four Seas Co., 1924.

Soldier's Pay (Novel). New York: Boni and Liveright, 1926.

Mosquitoes (Novel). New York: Boni and Liveright, 1927.

Sartoris (Novel). New York: Harcourt, Brace and World, 1929.

The Sound and the Fury (Novel). New York: Cape and Smith, 1929.

Sanctuary (Novel). New York: Cape and Smith, 1931.

These 13 (Stories). New York: Cape and Smith, 1931.

Light in August (Novel). New York: Smith and Haas, 1932.

A Green Bough (Poems). New York: Smith and Haas, 1933.

Doctor Martino and Other Stories. New York: Smith and Haas, 1934.

Pylon (Novel). New York: Smith and Haas, 1935.

Absalom, Absalom! (Novel). New York: Random House, 1936.

The Unvanquished (Novel). New York: Random House, 1938.

The Wild Palms (Novel). New York: Random House, 1939.

The Hamlet (Novel). New York: Random House, 1940.

Go Down, Moses, and Other Stories (Novel). New York: Random House, 1942.

Intruder in the Dust (Novel). New York: Random House, 1948.

Knight's Gambit: Stories. New York: Random House, 1949.

Requiem for a Nun (Novel). New York: Random House, 1951.

A Fable (Novel). New York: Random House, 1954.

Big Woods (Stories). New York: Random House, 1955.

The Town (Novel). New York: Random House, 1957.

The Mansion (Novel). New York: Random House, 1959.

The Reivers (Novel). New York: Random House, 1962.

Anthologies, Speeches, and Interviews

The Portable Faulkner. Malcolm Cowley, ed. New York: The Viking Press, 1946. A representative selection from Faulkner's prewar production, with an interesting introduction.

The Faulkner Reader. Saxe Communs, ed. New York: Random House, 1954. A more recent anthology.

Faulkner at Nagano. Robert A. Jeliffe, ed. Tokyo: The Kenkyusha Press, 1956. Transcript of speeches and conferences of Faulkner's Japanese lecture tour.

Faulkner in the University. Frederick L. Gwynn and Joseph L. Blotner, eds. Charlottesville: The University of Virginia Press, 1959. Record of Faulkner's years as writer-in-residence at University of Virginia.

Faulkner Bibliographies

Meriweather, James B. "William Faulkner: A Check List," *The Princeton University Library Chronicle,* XVII (Spring, 1957). The best available bibliography of Faulkner's works.

Vickery, Olga W. "A Selective Bibliography," *William Faulkner: Three Decades of Criticism.* East Lansing: The Michigan State University Press, 1960. This is the most useful list of criticism about Faulkner.

Sleeth, Irene Lynn. "William Faulkner: A Bibliography of Criticism," *Twentieth-Century Literature,* VIII (April, 1962). More complete than the work above, but some of the information given is inaccurate.

General Criticism, Biographies, and Reminiscences

Coughlan, Robert. *The Private World of William Faulkner.* New York: Harper & Bros., 1954. Informative introduction, with emphasis on the biographical side. Not useful as criticism.

Cullen, John B., in collaboration with Watkins, Floyd C. *Old Times in the Faulkner Country.* Chapel Hill: The University of North Carolina Press, 1961.

Faulkner, John. *My Brother Bill: An Affectionate Reminiscence.* New York: Trident Press, 1963. John Faulkner is William's younger brother. He has published a number of novels. The book is important as a biographical source work.

Fiedler, Leslie A. "William Faulkner: Highbrow's Lowbrow," *No, in Thunder!* Boston: Beacon Press, 1960. Faulkner from the viewpoint of an avant-garde critic.

Frohock, W. M. "William Faulkner: The Private Versus the Public Vision," *The Novel of Violence in America.* Dallas: Southern Methodist University Press, 1950.

Hoffman, Frederick J. *William Faulkner.* New York: Twayne Publishers, Inc., 1961. Stresses the major works and explains the peculiarities of Faulkner's style and method.

Hoffman, Frederick J. and Vickery, Olga W., eds. *William Faulkner: Three Decades of Criticism.* East Lansing: Michigan State University Press, 1960. A valuable anthology of criticism on Faulkner, selected by two scholars who are well acquainted with the field. A basic work for students writing terms papers on Faulkner.

Hopper, Vincent F. "Faulkner's Paradise Lost," *Virginia Quarterly Review,* XXIII.

Howe, Irving. *William Faulkner: A Critical Study.* New York: Random House, 1952. Available as a Vintage paperback in a revised and expanded edition, 1962. A good introduction, but not thorough criticism.

Longley, John Lewis, Jr. *The Tragic Mask: A Study of Faulkner's Heroes.* Chapel Hill: The University of North Carolina Press, 1963.

Malin, Irving. *William Faulkner: An Interpretation.* Stanford: Stanford University Press, 1957.

Millgate, Michael. *William Faulkner.* New York: Grove Press, 1961.

Miner, Ward L. *The World of William Faulkner.* Durham: Duke University Press, 1952. For the student wishing to do research on the real-life sources of the Yoknapatawpha books.

Nilon, Charles H. *Faulkner and the Negro*. Boulder: University of Colorado Press, 1962. Available as a Citadel Press paperback, 1965. An analysis of Faulkner's treatment of Negro characters.

O'Connor, William Van. *The Tangled Fire of William Faulkner*. Minneapolis: University of Minnesota Press, 1954. Informative, interesting, modern in approach.

———. *William Faulkner*. Minneapolis: University of Minnesota Press, 1959. One of the Pamphlets on American Writers series. Gives quick bird's eye view of Faulkner's works.

O'Donnell, George Marion. "Faulkner's Mythology," *Kenyon Review,* I.

Robb, Mary Cooper. *William Faulkner: An Estimate of His Contribution to the American Novel*. Pittsburgh: University of Pittsburgh Press, 1957.

Slatoff, Walter J. *Quest for Failure: A Study of William Faulkner*. Ithaca: Cornell University Press, 1960. Study of language usage.

Stein, Jean. "William Faulkner: An Interview." *Paris Review,* IV.

Swiggart, Peter. "Time in Faulkner's Novels," *Modern Fiction Studies,* V.

———. *The Art of Faulkner's Novels*. Austin: The University of Texas Press, 1962.

Thompson, Lawrence. *William Faulkner: An Introduction and Interpretation*. New York: Barnes & Noble, Inc., 1963.

Vickery, Olga W. *The Novels of William Faulkner: A Critical Interpretation*. Baton Rouge: Louisiana State University Press, 1959. A reliable work of scholarship.

Volpe, Edmond L. *A Reader's Guide to William Faulkner*. New York: The Noonday Press, 1964. The most complete and detailed guide to Faulkner's work so far. Very handy for the student as a general introduction. Carefully checked factual information, clearly stated criticism.

Waggoner, Hyatt H. *William Faulkner: From Jefferson to the World.* Lexington: University of Kentucky Press, 1959. A perceptive study, particularly good on *A Fable.*

On Faulkner's Technique

Campbell, Harry M. "Structural Devices in the Works of Faulkner," *Perspective,* III.

Riedel, F. C. "Faulkner as Stylist," *South Atlantic Quarterly,* LVI.

Slatoff, Walter J. "The Edge of Order: The Pattern of Faulkner's Rhetoric," *Twentieth-Century Literature,* III.

Hovde, Carl F. "Faulkner's Democratic Rhetoric," *South Atlantic Quarterly,* LXIII.

Zink, Karl E. "William Faulkner: Form as Experience," *South Atlantic Quarterly,* LIII.

On *Light In August*

Benson, Carl. "Thematic Design in *Light in August,*" *South Atlantic Quarterly,* LIII (October, 1954), 540–55.

Chase, Richard. "The Stone and the Crucifixion: Faulkner's *Light in August,*" *Kenyon Review,* X (Autumn, 1948), 539–51. One of the basic essays on the novel. Included in *Three Decades of Criticism.*

Cottrell, Beekman W. "Christian Symbols in *Light in August,*" *Modern Fiction Studies,* II (Winter, 1956–7), 207–13. On Christ-Christmas parallels.

Hoffman, Frederick J. *William Faulkner.* New York: Twayne Publishers, Inc., 1961, 69–73. See Critical Commentary.

Holman, C. Hugh. "The Unity of Faulkner's *Light in August,*" *PMLA,* LXXII (March, 1958), 155–66.

Kazin, Alfred. "The Stillness of *Light in August,*" *Twelve Original Essays,* Charles Shapiro, ed. Detroit: Wayne State University Press, 1958. See Critical Commentary.

Kimmey, John L. "The Good Earth in *Light in August,*" *Mississippi Quarterly,* XVII, 1–8. On character of Lena Grove.

Lind, Ilse Dusoir. "The Calvinistic Burden of *Light in August,*" *The New England Quarterly,* XXX (September, 1957), 307–29. On religious fanaticism as a motivation of the novel's characters.

Longley, John L. Jr. "Joe Christmas: The Hero in the Modern World," *Virginia Quarterly Review,* XXXII (Spring, 1957), 233–49. Discusses Christmas as alienated modern protagonist.

Nilon, Charles H. *Faulkner and the Negro.* New York: The Citadel Press, 1965, 73–93. See Critical Commentary.

O'Connor, William Van. "Protestantism in Yoknapatawpha County," *Hopkins Review,* V (Spring, 1952), 26–42.

On Other Novels by Faulkner

This section is arranged according to the alphabetical order of the novels, instead of the critics' names, to provide easier reference.

Brooks, Cleanth, *"Absalom, Absalom!:* The Definition of Innocence," *The Sewanee Review,* XIX.

Sullivan, Walter, "The Tragic Design of *Absalom, Absalom!*" *South Atlantic Quarterly,* L.

Pritchett, V. S., "Time Frozen," *Partisan Review,* XXI (On *A Fable*).

Straumann, Heinrich. "An American Interpretation of Existence: Faulkner's *A Fable,*" *Anglia,* LXXIII.

Lewis, R. W. B. "The Hero in the New World: William Faulkner's 'The Bear'," *Kenyon Review,* XIII.

Warren, Robert Penn. "The Snopes World," *Kenyon Review,* III (On *The Hamlet*).

Lytle, Andrew. "Regeneration for the Man," *The Sewanee Review,* LVII (On *Intruder in the Dust*).

Beck, Warren. "Faulkner in *The Mansion,*" *Virginia Quarterly Review,* XXXVI.

Torchiana, Donald T. "Faulkner's *Pylon* and the Structure of Modernity," *Twentieth-Century Literature,* IV.

Cole, Douglas. "Faulkner's *Sanctuary:* Retreat from Responsibility," *Western Humanities Review,* XIV.

Sartre, Jean-Paul. *"Sartoris," Literary and Philosophical Essays,* London: Rider, 1955.

Marcus, Steven. "Snopes Revisited," *Partisan Review,* XXIV (On the Snopes trilogy).

Bowling, Lawrence Edward. "Faulkner and the Theme of Innocence," *Kenyon Review,* XX (On *The Sound and the Fury*).

Cross, Barbara. *"The Sound and the Fury:* The Pattern of Sacrifice," *Arizona Quarterly,* XVI.

Lowrey, Perrin. "Concepts of Time in *The Sound and the Fury,*" *English Institute Essays,* 1952.

Sartre, Jean-Paul. "Time in Faulkner's *The Sound and the Fury*," *William Faulkner: Three Decades of Criticism*. East Lansing: Michigan State University Press, 1960.

Stewart, George R., and Backus, Joseph M., "Each in its Ordered Place: Structure and Narrative in Benjy's Section of *The Sound and the Fury*," *American Literature*, XXIX.

NOTES

NOTES

NOTES

NOTES

NOTES

NOTES

NOTES

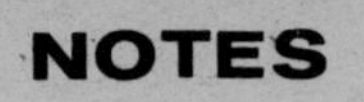
NOTES